With a Pocketful of Mint

Grace M Wells

"This is a wonderful representation of first loves and how sometimes good things must end. And sometimes, it's okay to linger a bit before moving on."

- Brooke Goodwin, Author of "Exposed" and "in this glass prism"

"[This book] is a journey that captures so many tiny feelings of memory and want and how those memories are both held close but are something bitter and unfinished... It's a beautiful journey of processing and sitting with heartbreak, moving on in a way that's healing."

- Caroline Hamel, Author of "To Hold a Flower"

"This book is amazing as always! A deep dive into the author's mind, and I'm here for every second!"

- Zion Gardner

Dedication

For those who struggle with letting go. For those who wish they would just come back. For those who want nothing more than to run back into their arms.

For those who put all of their wishes on stars they can't see.

For you.

And for Aidan.

The pen traces curves
Envisioned on the paper,
Letters form words,
Words form letters

From the very first "I know"
To the final "I love you",
Ink flows from page to page
Describing affection to only you

– Forming Letters

Part 1 – Back When

And yet
I never want to
Stop looking at
Old, faded memories
Taken while
The younger me
Wore her
Rose-colored glasses

- Photo Journals

I.
Just a teenager and her boyfriend
Walking back and forth through
The mall that's nearby;
The mall they rarely go to

No school books to be found,
Just pretzels and hot cocoa

II.
Songs played
Promises made
Fast-forward untouched
Lyric sheets scrunched
Endless loopback shone bright
Earbuds serenade all night

III.
Steps to sit on a
Bench, you turn and
Whisper to me, your
Watch is smooth, your
Hand finds mine, your
Flash is on, the
World is mute, the
Time has suspended so your
Eyes can search mine

- 3

The chocolate wrappers
that we held,
that you gave,
were flattened
folded
put in a box
and saved.

Every now and then
I open the box
Let the light shine on them,
Let them taint my brain.

- Godiva

Soup
Breadsticks
Fancy dresses
Getting dolled up
For high school dances

A boy
A girl
Two in the world
In a normal life
For just one night

– Starlights

The ridges of my fingerprints
Nerves in my skin
Kiss
You

— First Touch

With the strobe lights
When you held me
Because my life depended on it

- Halloween Night

Plastic chairs
Erasers
Small lunch box
Applesauce
Four McMuffins
Off-hand comments
Canceled plans
And a black pen

— That Morning

Fairy lights hanging from
Wooden beams
And bowls of crême brulée
And spoons and napkins
And a ring

- Andes Mints

Moving through the lights,
Eating food from the tables,
Standing on the sidelines,
Dancing when I'm able.

The bleachers fade to trees,
Tables into an old garage,
Gym floor changes to concrete,
And I just want to be
home.

- It Should've Been With You

I'm trying
So hard
To focus on cars
And talking of cars
But
We stopped at an ATM

– Under the Awning

Even my shadow longs for reprieve
From having to listen to my relentless repeats
Of our memories from long ago

— Ghost Stories

Part 2 — Pining

Each lightbulb glows
On the globe
Each second closer to the ground

They all feel like ghosts
No one knows
How I feel lonely on this full couch

Flutes sipping silently
Liquid bubbly
Can't hear you speak my name

Counting up to twenty
I'm not ready
Starting another 365 days

— New Year Missing You

The tune that brings me back
To the hope that I once had
Plays again on the same list of songs
That my sister repeats ad nauseam
Reminding me of past mistakes,
Montage of nothing but your face
Creating mixed feelings of pain and
Love and caution, hurt and hatred,
Endless futures and spending forever,
First dates, saving grace, second chances,
Being together

— March 18

I tried making a list once
Of the things that remind me of you

Music
Planes
Cantaloupe
Chocolate
Orange soda
Italian food

I filled the page up,
But it seemed too few

Mint
Crocodiles
Glow sticks
Gold
Watches
Walnuts

It was never enough, this list –
Too often I think of you

Giants
Traveling
Photography
Iceland
Lilies
Poetry

– One Page Isn't Enough

Whenever I hear
One of our songs
It feels like
I'm getting a big hug
From a ghost's mother

— Pictures and Bottles

I longed
To be the one
To write
Your love poems

To capture
Your beauty
With words

To live in your head
Like a song
Poisoning your brain
As you in mine

To boast to
The entire world
Of the treasure I held —
Of the joy I found

- To Write Your Love Poems

And every time the door opens
Or I hear a gate unlocking
I check to see if it might be you
Hoping you're the one to come walking
Into the room like you used to do
Used to put the biggest smile on my face

But the tens of miles
In between you and me
Comes along, crushes my daydreams,
Brings me to reality
And then I wonder
Do you still think of me?

- Tracing

The thoughts froze,
My eyes dozed,
My mind wandered
Through the open window,

But I have to tell you
How much I care.
I wish you were here,
Or I was there.

I long for you.
How I wish there were a way
And my time is cut short,
But I just want to say
I love you.

- Smudge

He doesn't provide the breath in my lungs
or keep my heart beating,
but
he makes it beat so much stronger.

He doesn't keep my brain turned on,
but
he provides the extra *spark*
of energy.

I *want* his presence.

When he's here,
everything is
beautiful
again.

When he talks to me,
the world
sings.

When he sits with me
in silence,
time embraces us.

When he looks at me,
he sees my soul —
I feel known.

He doesn't provide the breath in my lungs
but without him,
the world is
an empty cardboard box.

With him,
surviving
becomes
living.

— His Poem

Is this love?

Being caught up in feelings
Laughter in your eyes

Is this love?

Wanting you near me
Sweet, subtle smiles

Is this love?

Counting down minutes
Face full of blush

Is this love?

Dying for you to pick us
Dizzy head rush

Is this love?

Reliving memories
Longing for your touch

Is this love?

Letting you know me
Knowing too much

- I Think I Love You

You
Holding my hand
Listening to me
Singing me songs
Showing me love
Telling me about
Airplanes

Me
Talking to you
Sitting with you
Holding your hand
Knowing little things
Writing you
Poetry

— Revisiting

Poetry never
Spoke to your heart
And yet
You still cherished
The art –
The words
That I wrote –
That I shared –
That I spoke

You called me yours
And my poetry followed

– Your Type of Love

It's funny.
It seems that the
Rest of the world is
Blind to your beauty,
Tone-deaf to your melody,
Immobile in the midst
Of your rhythmic flow.

– Can't Stop My Feet

Every thought
That brings a smile to my face
Is of
You

— On My Mind

63,072,000 moments in time
Lost, spent, shared, memorized,

And I let greed
Get the better of me
Because I'm always left wanting
One moment more

- Happy Anniversary

You like Hamilton
You remember my favorite things
You tried a love poem
You sampled my interests
You gave a helping hand
You gave your heart
You understand me

You knew me before
You left

– October

1 year of payment
For a sliver of a chance for change
But even if it cost me 30,
My answer would still be the same

- I Choose You

Organize, label,
Put everything in its place,
No longer trying to forget,
No longer trying to erase,

And there is happiness
In the airports,
In the chocolate,
In the song lyrics.

To share a lifetime
Is truly a gift.

— Peace

Part 3 — Lonely

I'm trapped
I miss our past
But our future
Is what I miss most

Remembering
Isn't the hard thing
It's knowing that
You want me

But we're still caught
A thousand miles apart
Wanting a word or two
Wishing for a moment

— Hopelessly

When I asked to forget,
This is not what I meant.

- Recall

Let me forget the lack of replies
Let me forget "goodbye"
Don't let me forget the twinkle
  I used to see in his eyes

Don't let me forget his voice
  saying sweet nothings in my ear
Don't let me forget his hands holding mine
  as I cry into his shoulder

Don't let me forget the way
  he'd light up every room he walked into
Don't let me forget the times
  he'd whisper to me, "I love you"

Let me forget the lonely days
Let me forget the pain
Don't let me forget him

– Not Like This

I want you so much.

I only wish
I was more than the
Ghost of which
You once remembered,
And that you
Were more than
A glimmer
From my imagination –
A sliver of hope I once had.

– In the Past

You'll be happier without me.

Be happy
That you're free

- Be Happy, Be Free

It's been 180 days
And all I can still see
Is the way the A in your name
Never changed

- A

It's such a simple word
No one thinks about it
They just say it

I didn't used to think about it
I used to just say it

And now it's more than a word
To me
It's something that stands out
It's a knife
A spike
An irregularity
A noticeable change
A shift only I can sense
With this weird seventh sense

No one talks about this sense,
But I'm sure we all have it
We all have little things
That make us stop
And make us think
And make us pause and overthink
And break down the skeleton underneath
The skin we wear as a shield
To keep us from feeling these things
From the knives, the spikes they wield
Disguised as simple words

— **Rock**

The stars hang there
Waiting their turn,
They're too far away
To hear the words
I speak to myself
But long to speak to you,
You're too far away too

And though a million miles
And mountains keep us
Apart,
I know that
There can be — there is
A hope for the unknown
Possibility of renewal
Chance at something new

But knowledge turns to thoughts,
Hopes turn to daydreams,
Thoughts and daydreams turn
Into ignored scenes
And string-shaped images
And panic every which way…

I thought you'd stay

— Infinity

I hate sleep
Because I want to live
In the world of dreams
Where you still love me

I guess I should say
I hate waking up

– Never To Wake

Hallucinating
Conversations,
Imagining
Relationships,
Non-existent
Exchanges.

- Waiting for a Ghost

Trying to choose
Which blurry figures
Across the way
Look most like you

– **Visions**

I keep checking the driver's seat
Of every white SUV,
And I look over my shoulder
Hoping to maybe see
You —
Catch a hold of your eye,
A glimpse of your smile,
A trigger to push me back in time,
But I'm at the front of the line
And the trigger is aimed at my neck
Tick, tick,
Clicking sounds
Fill my head,
And the brakes are sliced.
No matter how hard I try,
I can't find you out among them.

And can I say
How many times
I've stopped and almost —
In the pull of a wild emotional tide —
Turned the wheel to
Take me by
Your house
So maybe I can see you
One last time before you
Slip away from me,
Back down the cracks
No more "Stuck Like Glue" painting pictures,
Just pitch black
And heart attacks
And giving in,
And giving up.
Where did I put my trust?
Where did I put the ticket stubs
From our first date?
When was the day I made my first mistake?
Can I fix the problems I've managed to create?
Can I erase the days you were down at the bay,
And the one just before New Year's day?

You won't hold me like that again,
And I'll never forget it…

But that's my problem, see
My friends, they hate me
Bringing up a side of you that they've never
seen.
They talk,
They laugh,
They tell me to shush up,
They tell me to take your hoodie and stuff it
Back in the drawer, since you won't take it
back
But little do they know that that
Hoodie is sometimes all I can grab.
My cling to reality,
My division from fiction.

It still smells like you.
After all it's been through,
It still smells like you.

- Let Me Sleep

I cover myself in lime
To smother the scent

Of sweat –
Of warm summer days
Walking through town

Of nausea –
Of sugary sweets
Too sweet to eat at once

Of metal –
Of hinges on
Brand new watches

Of plastic –
Of glasses
Far too big for my face

Of pork –
Of messy sandwiches
And eating at tables

Of ink –
Of fresh paper
Hot off the printer

Of popcorn –
Of movie dates
Spent in comfortable silence

Of stone –
Of the real tiles
On his hall floor

Of cotton –
Of cozy nights
Forgetting about life for a minute

– Made of This

Questions without answers.
Can silence be taken?
It's always manipulated
Into meanings unlimited
With no recollection
Of reality checks,
And cloudy flecks
Of misjudgement,
Are never stirred
And words never heard
By the brick wall
Obstacle
Until I slowly fall

- Dreams

Setting out
To new adventures,
Fading the scars
On my wrists,
Behind bushes, crouching
Compasses turn
Searching for stars,
And race to the finish

— Ambition (Part I)

And all along
My feet wanted to turn,
Run into your arms,
Take me back the 300 steps,
To before our song
And before the hurt
But I look forward, stay strong,
And find my future ahead

- **Yearning (Part II)**

Part 4 — Struggles

Her heart clenched in a way
She hadn't felt in a long time
As her memories came flooding back
Of what her life once was
And what she lost
The day she let nothing
Hold her back.

– Tiny Reminders

Scaring off the fish,
Or losing my grip on the rod;
Either way, I can lose
The one thing in my life that I love.

— **Something to Say**

I don't know
Why you left
Who took you away
Or what thoughts entered your head

But I know
When you left
I wasn't the same
I could never go back to the same
And the way things had been

— Suddenly

What if I hadn't underappreciated
The fleeting moments spent with you?
What if I hadn't thought only
Of my lack of your time
Instead of the gift of you?

What if I had spoken up sooner?
What if I hadn't said anything at all?
What if I left things how they were,
In pieces?
What if I let myself take the whole fall?

What if I had known
What I now know?
What if I could've had
More time with you
Rather than being
Confused and alone?

What if I knew
What I have to sacrifice?
What if...

— **"What if"s Too Late**

If it all came back
To me this day
In the future, from the past
And I had let another way
Grab a hold and pull me back
Then maybe you would've stayed.

- Wish I Had a Time Machine

We were walking
  this tightrope
I held your hand

"Don't look down,"
  I said
You didn't listen

You returned
  to the start
Before we began

Now I'm here
  on this wire
Just sitting

*Waiting for you
  to come back
And be with me again*

– Heights

These dreams
Are starting to feel
Lonely

These doubts
Condense my frail
Anxiety

These days
I'm hoping that you
Miss me

- Broken Heart

When I had, I didn't know
When I knew, I couldn't have

When you love, don't let her go,
Just hold on to every moment you get

— Passenger

But none of them know
About wishing at midnight
About the secret conversations
And staying up late
About the things that you told me
And the things that we said

About the feelings I got
During movie days
About the list of notes
That we shared just us two

None of them know
The secrets of you

- Secrets

And in the morning,
   the air will be fresh
   and cool again
But for now I'm stuck
   in this stuffy room
   rereading the last words you said

The past seems so written in stone
But I barely remember picking up a chisel

Now I'm frozen here on the dark couch
Here with all the lights out
In the middle of the night and it's black
outside
Don't remember if I cried
But I know that I died
Just a little

Delusional fantasy
Imagination daydream
For you, everything
Worked out so perfectly

You've probably moved on
Found a way to heal your heart
But I'm locked inside a vault
And I'm reaching out my arms
Squeezing in between the bars
And I know it's all my fault

How I miss being in your arms

– Ten Feet Underground

Part 5 – Relearning

Cutting off the circulation
Leaving red marks
But after the release,
It still won't matter
If there was harm or good –
The imprint still remains,
It still feels like there's something missing
A phantom presence lingering

– Strangulation

As fast as a hummingbird
Beats its wings upon its breast
Is how fast I fall for you

Yet you throw me away

— A Thousand Moments

Can we finally agree
That we are better
When either we
Are together
Or not? Because this back and forth
Thing that we have —
It exhausts me.
I'm tired,
And I've just about had
Enough.

I'm okay
With being alone.
I have a place of my own
To call home,
And I'm fine staying here
Independent...

- Even Though I Want You

Saying "I love you"
Isn't leaving me to
Fend for myself
Against the demons running races
In my head.

Saying "I love you"
Is everything you used to do
Before you left.

— Actions Speak Louder

Working and reworking
Kneading the clay
Fire in the kiln
Rough patches

- Pottery Heart

Part 6 — Hopeful

One is for youth
And naïve beliefs,
One is for our love
And the simpler dreams,
One is for self-love
And healing from heartbreak,
One is for renewals
And forgiving old mistakes,
One is for forever
And brand new beginnings,
One is for me and you
And stories with happy endings.

- **Silver Reminders**

It's hard because
Everyone knows
And at the same time
No one knows

- **Our Heartbreak**

I'm not sad that it ended
I've come to learn to accept
death
As a necessary part of being
alive

dark
Is necessary to have
light

However, I mourn the premature loss of
what could've been

- A Picket Fence

And I wonder
If you ever end up
Driving past my house,
Because in a land
So wide as ours
It's hard to believe
Your path
Ever crossed mine

- Fate

I'd say I feel safe in your arms
But it's more than that

Because in your arms,
I feel like I'm *allowed* to be safe
I'm *allowed* to take a minute
To relax
To let it all go
To sleep peacefully

I'm allowed to *rest*

– Reflections

Part 7 – Anticipating

"I'm sorry.
I'm so sorry
For breaking your heart,
For getting your hopes up
After you'd already given up,
For making a promise
I intended to keep
But going and
Breaking it instead,
For letting the
Words in my head
Drive both of us insane,
For shifting blame,
For acting on impulse,
For caring too much,
For not caring enough,
For being so doubtful
And insecure
And thinking that
You'd be better off without me,
For crushing your spirits and dreams.

"You probably felt how I did
On that night so long ago.
I wish I could've told you in person,
And now I get the chance
To right the wrongs I made in the past
And fix my mistakes.
Do you want the same?
Do you want my closure,
Or to just walk away?

"Are you thankful it's over,
There's no more crazy girl at your shoulder,
Or do you wish that I would've stayed?"

— If I Ever See You Again

Did you see it?
Did you read it?
I couldn't admit it
Through anything but words
That your love put in my head
And your pain put in my heart
But don't worry,
The pleasant dreams on the edge
By the fire's hearth
Return to me.
After everything,
The pain you caused me...

Doesn't hurt.

- I Wrote You a Poem

I know what I'll do –
I imagine it every night
Trying to perfect the plan
So everything goes just right:

I'll run up and hug you
Like never before,
And I'll be on my tip-toes
Because I'm so short.

I'll finally be able
To see your eyes smiling at me,
And heaven will be on earth once more
When you stand in front of me.

– On That Night (I)

Such a funny
Ironic
Coincidence
That we should first meet again
In the same place
That we once
Stood in line,
Held hands,
Ate lunch,
Made jokes,
Walked,
Spoke,
Existed.

– Our Favorite Spot (II)

I ordered a salad
with olives
tomatoes
and extra pineapples

You were waiting
for your pizza

I paid at the counter
and got a cup
for a soft drink
but your favorite cake wasn't there

You stared
at the wall

I walked past to get
orange soda
like always
to pretend I'm alright

You didn't move
a single inch

I could feel you
staring at me
at the back of my head

– Not Like Before (III)

Did you have to
Hold yourself back
From reaching out
And touching me
When I walked by
Too?

- That Night At Dinner (IV)

Part 8 — Patience

So I sat here
Making clover chains
Waiting for the day

Patience spilling over
Losing drops
'Til it stopped
And I got up to take a break

I spent so long pacing
From one side to the other
And I never know quite what to think
Never know to wonder
If you're ever coming back
Or if it'll break my heart too much
And shatter it like glass
On the cold pavement
Where you left me

I'm just waiting
Making clover chains
And I want to pretend it's okay
'Cause even though I don't know,
I'll be waiting

- Tiny Clovers

I'll never grow tired
Of waiting for you
To catch up
At your own pace.
I gave up
The chase
Because you can't race after
What's falling behind
Pausing
For a moment

— Resting

Maybe
"Letting go"
Isn't
"Moving on"

It's saying
"I'll keep my ear out for your voice calling my
name."

– Letting Go

For now, I will make myself content
With sitting and being patient

— **Content**

And I know I could be
More patient and calm,
And I could try to feel better
And try to move on,

But if you're willing to try,
I've made myself better.
You know how to find me —
If you want me, I'm here.

- Your Compass

Part 9 — Closure

I always wished for a second chance with you

All I ever got was
Smoke and mirrors,
Fake commitments,
Double-edged swords,
And a heart broken too many times.

– Second Chances

I can't believe
I had let
The faint memory of
Holding hands
Turn grass strands
Into iron bars
Locking me in
The past

— 2 Years Ago

If I didn't have you,
  then I wouldn't know what I want.
If I didn't have you,
  then I wouldn't have grown into
  the person I was meant to become.
If I didn't have you,
  I would have ruined every relationship
  that I tried to get into.
If I didn't have you,
  I wouldn't have ever realized that
  some people are meant to
  only be in your life for a season.
If I didn't have you,
  I would've never learned how to let myself
  enjoy being treated right.
If I didn't have you,
  I would've never learned how to
  forgive myself.
If I didn't have you,
  I would've never learned how to escape
  the past.

- Teaching Moments

It's taken two years
Two long, excruciating years
But I did it
I found it

- **Happy**

I wanted to write
A thousand books
About how I felt
About you.

Now I realize
Those feelings
Were blind from the truth.

I want to write
A thousand books
About how I feel,
And about you.

Now I realize
There's a difference
Between the two.

- You Stopped Loving Me

I have a new muse.
He gives me
White daisies and
Star-filled skies,
Moonlight shadows and
Firesides,
Warm spring rolls and
Wondrous eyes,
Contagious smiles and
Cozy nights.

- New Light

Afterword

Thank you so much for reading my fifth collection of poetry! After publishing "On a Tuesday in April", I realized that I still had so many more poems left. I had to create another poetry book with a similar theme: grieving a heartbreak.

These poems are still all about my first love, but this book focuses more on the afterward feelings rather than the feelings I experienced while in the relationship. It's all about looking back on the relationship with the knowledge that I have today.

It's very important to recognize and acknowledge these feelings without shoving them away in a box. When you're grieving, you need to let yourself feel what you feel in order to effectively move on.

I hope that you never have to feel this sort of loss again, but if you do, you're not alone. You will never be alone.

Feel free to chat with me on Instagram @gmwells_author, email me at gmwellsbooks@gmail.com, or get in contact with me in another way to tell me what you think, or just to talk! I love hearing from my readers because I get to make new connections with people.

Thank you all. Thank you for reading my poems, and above all thank you for coming along on this long, wavy journey. I hope to see you again soon.

—Gracie

Acknowledgments

Thank you to all of my poetry buddies. You guys have been so essential in the creation of my books! Between feedback, encouragement, and just general support, I definitely would not be able to do this without you guys.

Thank you to my amazing beta readers who work to give me feedback and make sure that the books I publish are the absolute best. I could not have done any of this work as an author without the incredible help of Brooke Goodwin, Serena Morrigan, Kelly Ottiano, Ben Koenig, Zion Gardner, and Caroline Hamel.

Thank you to Cyrena for listening to my stories, for dancing with me, and for making me cry (in a good way) at our sleepover. Thank you to Amber for still giving me the best advice and for giving me another shoulder to lean on. Thank you to Alyssa for continuing to be there for me through it all.

And a huge thank you to everyone who has supported my writing business! Thanks to you, I have been able to continue writing and putting my best efforts into publishing what I produce.

Want to read more books from Grace Wells?

Visit her website to get your own copy of "On a Tuesday in April"!

"On a Tuesday in April" by Grace M Wells

"[Grace] deserves more recognition with a book like this!"

– Brooke Goodwin; Author of "Exposed" and "in this glass prism"

"To anyone considering purchasing, don't hesitate for one second. This is beautifully done!"

– Haley Lombard

"Grace Wells' poetry is once again so simply beautiful and poignant that you feel everything without having to try ... I cannot recommend [this book] enough."

– Caroline Hamel; Author of "To Hold a Flower"

And look for these other titles by Grace Wells!

"2/23" by Grace M Wells

"Broken" by Grace M Wells

"Abyss" by Grace M Wells

"Surreal" by Grace M Wells

Like reading Grace Wells?

Here's what Grace Wells likes reading:

"To Walk on Moonbeams"
by Zombear Writes

"in this glass prism"
by Brooke Goodwin

"A Song for Every Scar"
by Serena Morrigan

"no matter the wreckage"
by Sarah Kay

"Poems"
by Elizabeth Bishop

"The Complete Poems of Emily Dickinson"
edited by Thomas H Johnson

Love this book? Don't forget to leave a review!

I just want to thank you SO MUCH for taking the time to read my book. This project was extremely exciting for me to complete.

I want to hear what you have to say about "With a Pocketful of Mint", so don't forget to leave a review! Every review matters, and it matters a lot! Just head on over to Goodreads, Amazon, or wherever you purchased this book to leave a review for me.

Thank you so much!

—Gracie

Would you like to see more poetry? Learn
something interesting? Maybe hear from me
every once in a while?

Sign up for my newsletter and check out my
website!

https://gmwells.weebly.com

ALSO

Follow my Instagram account
(@gmwells_author) for recent updates and
other tidbits!

And don't hesitate to reach out to me in
any way... I love hearing from you!